ab
.48

Why Frogs are Wet

Splash! This is what you hear when you walk along the edge of a pond. Frogs are jumping into the water. They may stay there until you go away.

Frogs are amphibians: they can live on the land and in the water. This partly explains why they are wet — but only partly. There are other reasons why frogs are always wet.

This book takes a closer look at frogs: their impressive ancestry, their fishlike infancy, their distinctive song, their phenomenal ability to jump, and the way they catch insects by flicking their sticky tongues out and in, faster than the eye can detect.

An experienced author and teacher, Judy Hawes writes about frogs with clarity and genuine interest. The pictures, by Don Madden, augment the text in a properly puckish spirit.

Why Frogs are Wet

By Judy Hawes

illustrated by Don Madden

A Harper Trophy Book

Thomas Y. Crowell   New York

LET'S-READ-AND-FIND-OUT BOOKS

Let's-Read-and-Find-Out Books are edited by Dr. Roma Gans, Professor Emeritus of Childhood Education, Teachers College, Columbia University, and Dr. Franklyn M. Branley, Astronomer Emeritus and former Chairman of the American Museum–Hayden Planetarium. Text and illustrations for each of the more than 100 books in the series are checked for accuracy by an expert in the relevant field. Other titles available in paperback are listed below. Look for them at your local bookstore or library.

Why Frogs are Wet

rogs were here on this earth before people. They
were here before monkeys, or cats.

Frogs were here before giraffes. Frogs have been
here for millions of years. And frogs are still with
us.

Long before there were frogs, there were fish. The fish breathed through their gills. After a long time, new kinds of fish appeared. These new fish had lungs for breathing.

They could live out of water for a little while. When
their ponds dried up, they were able to flop about
on land. They had to flop because they had no legs.
Later, some of the fish grew legs in place of fins. Now
they could move on land or in the water. These
were forefathers of our first frogs.

A frog can live in the water and on the land. It is called an "amphibian." "Amphibian" means "having a double life."

The frog has a wet skin. The wet skin holds the secret of his double life. The frog breathes through the pores in his skin. He also breathes through his lungs.

Under water a frog breathes through his skin. He takes air out of the water. On land a frog breathes through his lungs and his skin. But he can breathe through his skin only when the skin is wet. He cannot get enough air through his lungs alone. If the skin dries out, the pores close and the frog cannot breathe. The frog dies.

A frog's skin is always fresh. He sheds his skin often.
The frog eats the old skin. A fresh, new, wet skin
has already grown under the old.

In the fall and winter frogs dig into the mud under streams and ponds. They go to sleep for the winter. As soon as frogs wake in the spring from their long sleep, they hunt for mates.

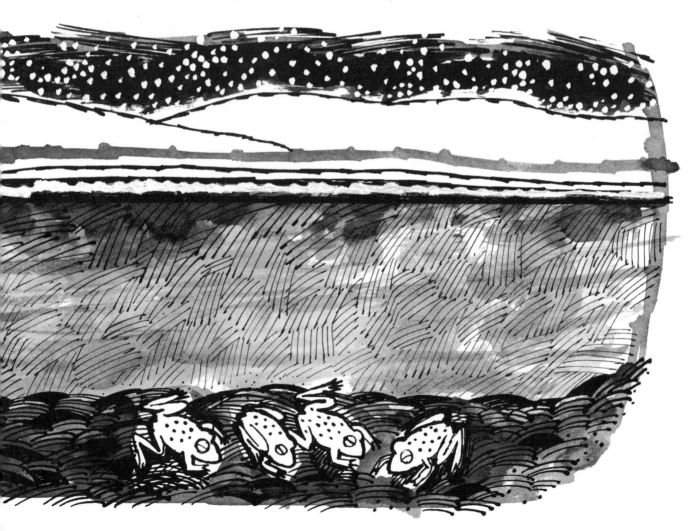

The female frogs lay thousands of eggs in the water. The male frogs fertilize them. A clump of eggs looks like a large helping of tapioca pudding. The eggs hatch in four to twenty-one days.

Frog babies, just hatched, are called tadpoles or pol-
liwogs. They look and swim like fish. They breathe
through gills like fish.

The gills look like fingers on each side of the tadpole's head. After a few days the gills disappear. Then you can see hind legs growing. Next the front legs appear. The tail is slowly taken into the body. Lungs for breathing on land take the place of gills. Now the little frog is an amphibian. He can live on land or in the water.

Some kinds of frogs live all their lives in water. Others live in woods or marshland. But all frogs return to the water to mate and lay their eggs. If they cannot find a pond, they may lay their eggs in a puddle!

There are more than two thousand kinds of frogs.
They are found all over the world. All of them
have wet skin. Most frogs are green, but there are
frogs of almost every color.

There are big frogs and little frogs. A giant frog lives in Africa. It is twelve inches long, not counting its legs. The largest frog in America is the bullfrog. It is six to eight inches long. The smallest in America is a tree frog. It is only half an inch long.

Frogs were the first creatures on earth to have voices. They use them when they hunt for a mate in the spring. The voices of bullfrogs are deep and low. They seem to say "jug 'o rum!" Tree frogs have a high-pitched song. It rings like distant bells. When they sing, their throats look like blown-up balloons. Other frog calls are grunts, squeaks, or squawks. Most female frogs do not sing, but they scream when they are frightened.

Frogs are great jumpers. They can leap ten, twenty, or thirty times their body length. They jump very fast and in zigzags.

The frog jumps to get away from his enemies and he jumps to catch his food.

When he looks for food, the frog does not jump about
foolishly. He waits, motionless, for insects to fly
within striking distance. He may sit on a branch,
a lily pad, or a rock, or he may float in the water.

His big, bulging eyes can see in all directions. Frogs stare without blinking. They can rest their eyes by shutting them half way. They can still see because they can look right through their lower eyelids.

Frogs jump after anything that seems to be a living, moving insect. If the insect stops moving, the frog will pay no attention to it. Frogs will starve before they will eat dead bugs.

When the frog's staring eyes spot a victim within striking distance, he leaps into action. The frog's tongue makes the catch. It seldom misses.

Frogs' tongues are different from ours. The frog's tongue is attached to the front of his mouth. It folds back toward his throat.

As a frog jumps for an insect, his tongue flips forward. The far end of the tongue is forked and has a sticky surface. This forked end wraps around the insect. The insect sticks to the tongue. Before the frog finishes his jump, his tongue swings back into his mouth. It throws the insect down his throat. All this takes less than a tenth of a second.

Frogs catch insects in water, near water, and on land. They come out to find food at twilight or on rainy and cloudy days. During the heat of the day they hide under damp leaves or under the water. They have to keep their skin wet because they are amphibians.

Never forget that frogs are amphibians. They can live in the water or on land. But only so long as their skin stays wet!

ABOUT THE AUTHOR

Mrs. Hawes, mother of four, has worked with children as a teacher and as a leader in scouting and Sunday school. She now teaches a public school class for handicapped children. A native of Forest Hills, New York, she was graduated from Vassar College. Mrs. Hawes and her husband are residents of Glen Rock, New Jersey, where they participate in many community activities.

She is the author of five other titles in the Let's-Read-and-Find-Out science series: *Bees and Beelines*, *Fireflies in the Night*, *Watch Honeybees with Me*, *Shrimps*, and *Ladybug, Ladybug, Fly Away Home*.

ABOUT THE ILLUSTRATOR

Don Madden has always loved animals and the outdoors. He is delighted, therefore, to be living in an old house in upstate New York, surrounded by acres of wild country. Mr. Madden's illustrations often involve animal life and so he frequently uses the facilities of the American Museum of Natural History in New York City to augment both his photographic files and personal knowledge.

Mr. Madden attended the Philadelphia Museum College of Art on a full scholarship. After graduation he joined the faculty as an instructor in experimental drawing and design. A recipient of gold and silver medals at exhibitions of the Philadelphia Art Director's Club, Mr. Madden has had his work reproduced in the New York Art Director's Annual and in the international advertising art publication *Graphis*.